BOLD IDEAS: THE INVENTOR'S GUIDE TO PATENTS

BoldPatents.com 800-849-1913 info@boldip.com

Bold Ideas: The Inventor's Guide to Patents

J.D. Houvener

Patent Attorney and Founder of:
Bold IP, PLLC

BoldPatents.com 800-849-1913 info@boldip.com

Printed in the United States of America

First Printing: March, 2016
Create Space, Inc. a division of Amazon, Inc.

ISBN-13: 9780692633205
ISBN-10: 0692633200

NOTICE:

This book is not legal advice.
There is no attorney-client relationship formed.

BoldPatents.com 800-849-1913 info@boldip.com

Smooth Sailing

Congratulations! By reading this, you've already taken the first step toward protecting and monetizing your **bold** ideas. As you probably know, there is an absolute sea of information out there about Patents on the internet. Like so many other inquiries made online, the question becomes not whether there is any information on the subject, but "which source of information can I trust?" and "who can I talk to about *my* specific invention?" and even more, "why do I have to pay an attorney $500/hour to get some simple questions answered?"

Well, let me take up the last question first. Quite simply, many attorneys justify charging clients for educating them on the patent process. And while I get it, some people are willing to pay that kind of money, the majority are not. And the majority of solo inventors that I have come across in my practice are not either. What this means is that inventors will try to save money by trying to learn on their own before approaching an attorney. They will seek out blogs, online journals, and articles and read through case law or other legal books. Because there is so much misinformation, opinion-based articles, these inventors either become confused or form an incorrect understanding of the law. By the time I get to speak with some of these clients, there is quite a bit of unraveling, clarifying and de-mystifying what they attempted to learn and do on their own.

I've found that once I'm able to give the client the straightforward answers they've been looking for, calm them down, and show them the process and path forward, it's smooth sailing. Teaching clients is something that comes with the job, but my passion is practicing the law and helping clients navigate their case through the USPTO. This means that the less time I spend teaching them about the basics, the better job I can do.

If a client came in with a clear understanding of the patent process, had clear expectations and knew how they could help, the stronger the potential for both invention and creator. When the client is on the same page as I am in the process, I am able to focus on what counts and they get the most out of my time, so it costs less! It's a true win-win. So, it is my goal that through this book, more inventors *and* attorneys will sail smoothly through their Patenting process.

TABLE OF CONTENTS

Smooth Sailing v

Section 1 "Us Patents: Definitions & Patentability" . . . 1

Chapter 1 What is a Patent? 3

Chapter 2 Why Should I Obtain a Patent? 7

Chapter 3 What Types of Innovations Can Obtain a Patent? 9

Chapter 4 Are Ideas Patentable? 13

Chapter 5 The Heart of Patent Eligibility 16

Chapter 6 Utility, Novelty, and Non-Obviousness 18

Chapter 7 Patent Claims and the Tangibility of Digital Products 21

Section 2 "Obtaining a Patent: The Four Basic Steps" 25

Chapter 8 Step One: Preliminary Patentability Search 27

Chapter 9 Step Two: Hire a Registered Patent Attorney. 30

Chapter 10 Step Three: Estimate Application Costs. 35

Chapter 11 The Patent Application Checklist . . . 42

Chapter 12 Step Five: Examiner Review. 47

Chapter 13 Step Six: Application Maintenance . . 52

Section 3 "How It Works: Rights and Infringement" . . 55

Chapter 14 Provisional vs. Non-Provisional Applications 57

Chapter 15 The Three Major Patent Types 60

Chapter 16 Patent Expiration Dates. 65

BoldPatents.com 800-849-1913 info@boldip.com

Chapter 17 Foreign Patent Rights. 67

Chapter 18 Monetize Your Patent. 70

Chapter 19 The Basics of Enforcement 74

Chapter 20 Infringement and Intent 77

Chapter 21 Why Cease-and-Desist Letters Matter. . 80

Chapter 22 Patent Trolls: Problems and Solutions. 83

Section 4 "Additional Guidance for Potential Applicants" 87

Chapter 23 What is the difference between Patent Protection and Trade Secret Protection? 89

Chapter 24 Why Should Inventors with New Innovations Contact A Patent Attorney NOW? 96

Chapter 25 Responsible Disclosure 100

Chapter 26 Patentability Analysis Timeline 104

Chapter 27 Additional Resources 109

SECTION 1

"US PATENTS: DEFINITIONS & PATENTABILITY"

BoldPatents.com 800-849-1913 info@boldip.com

CHAPTER 1

WHAT IS A PATENT?

A patent is the core legal protection for inventors and their inventions. The purpose of this protection is to provide an inventor with the necessary time and space to make, use and sell his or her invention without the threat of competition. In essence, it is the right to exclude others, for a specified time period, from simultaneously building, using or selling that particular invention in the market place.

In exchange, the government—specifically the United States Patent and Trademark Office or (USPTO), requires that the inventor, using written descriptions, or through pictures, diagrams, figures, and drawings, disclose in intricate detail the precise way to make and use the invention he or she wishes to patent.

The patent office then tests the invention using the disclosed instructions and information. They recruit a hypothetical Person of Ordinary Skill in the Art POSTIA for short

To illustrate, let's say there is an invention currently under review for automobile motors and engines. The chosen POSITA would be an average automotive engineer. For the invention to qualify, the hired engineer would need to be able to pick up that patent application, read it, and know exactly how to go build and use it.

As the owner of a US patent, one can exclude others from copying, recreating, or offering to sell their invention in the United States. It's almost as though one were granted a temporary monopoly. Not only is the inventor guaranteed to be the only one legally allowed to use that particular invention—whether publicly or privately—they are also the only one that is able to sell the invention in the United States.

Other Types of Intellectual Property

While the scope of this book focuses on the patent, there are actually four (4) main types of Intellectual Property (IP) protection.

1. Patent
2. Trademark
3. Copyright
4. Trade Secret

To better understand the patent, we will first need to understand the difference between it and the three other types of IP protection.

TRADEMARK

A trademark is a designation of a good, or service, used to notify a customer, or potential customer, of precisely what good, or service they can expect to receive when they see that mark associated with its sale or advertisement.

A good example of a famous trademark is the Nike Swoosh. If that mark, the swoosh, appears on an article or clothing or a pair of shoes, for example, that product is immediately recognized as part of the Nike brand.

Trademarks can be powerful symbols in the marketplace, as it both instantly represents the manufacturer (and its reputation) as well as informs the consumer. Therefore, the very essence of trademark law is to help prevent confusion in the market place. If someone were to open up a Steakhouse and use two golden arches as part of its logo or on any advertising, the public may erroneously construe that this restaurant might be affiliated with McDonald's Restaurants.

Not that the owners of this Steakhouse necessarily intended to steal McDonald's already built up customer traction, but that it could. If a consumer cannot trust that a logo or mark is legally protected, the less the value of the mark.

COPYRIGHT

The tenets of copyright law are designed to protect creative works. "Creative work" is a broad category indeed. This is the artist's domain. Paintings, drawings, sketches, sculptures, books, be they fiction or nonfiction, and music, are all basic examples of IP that can be protected by a copyright.

To obtain a copyright, however, the work has to be "fixed in a tangible means." In short, it has to be published somehow. If the work is virtual, it could be "fixed" in an MP3 file. It could be a wave file, or it could be more traditional, such as a film reel, or a VHS tape, cassette, CD, book, etc. This recording or publication and its concomitant rights in the marketplace are then protected by the copyright designation.

TRADE SECRET

Trade secret law, though enforced under state, rather than federal law, protects any proprietary methods or formulae of a company or an individual that have immediate, economic value to competitors.

For instance, a well-known trade secret is the Coca-Cola recipe. The formula for the popular beverage, how to get its precise flavor, the chemicals used, the mixture, the heats, the treatments, etc. are all protected under a trade secret designation. Even the delivery and packaging can be considered part of a trade secret. Value brands, such as RC or Safeway would love to know Coke's formula. This an important protection, preventing companies from potentially stealing another's method and undercutting or destroying the value of the company that it was stolen from.

CHAPTER 2

WHY SHOULD I OBTAIN A PATENT?

So, one may say, "Sure, getting a patent seems cool and all, but why not just build, test and start selling my invention right away?"

In truth, there are MANY advantages to patent protection. Here are two (2) CRUCIAL reasons:

1. **Commerce.** A patent gives the inventor the right to stop others from manufacturing, copying, selling or importing the patented goods without permission of the patent holder, who retains EXCLUSIVE commercial rights. That's a big deal for a business or individual looking to monetize their invention. It enables them to avoid competition and really corner the market at a premium price point for the value that they deliver.
2. **Progress.** One of the other more altruistic reasons for patenting is the potential contribution to the world at large. Inventions advance medical

science, biotechnology, engines, chemicals, computers...need I go on?

Being required to disclose the intimate details of the invention means the inventor adds new information to the general, technical knowledge-base. To put it another way, the word gets out: someone invents a brand new way to build a combustion engine in Seattle and publishes it. A short while later, someone in Florida reads that patent and is able to start tinkering and then build out the next version of, or an upgrade to, the engine that was described and depicted in the patent from Seattle. This is how we progress as a country and as a people.

Did you know?

Patents are considered so valuable that the concept for them was put right into the constitution! Article 1, Section 8, Clause 8 provides for Congress to "promote the progress of science and useful arts, by securing for limited times to authors and inventors the exclusive right to their respective writings and discoveries..." (U.S. Const. art. I, § 8, cl. 8).

CHAPTER 3

What Types of Innovations Can Obtain a Patent?

According to the patent statute, "Any person who invents or discovers any new and useful process, machine, manufacture, or composition of matter, or any new and useful improvement thereof, may obtain a patent[1]."

Well, that all sounds like a lot of legalese. Let's get right to the nuts and bolts of that answer's meaning.

A complete, in-depth description of any actual machine, manufacture and composition of matter, or even "any useful improvement thereof," goes beyond the scope of this book.

However, to give you an idea as to how each type is defined, we will discuss what the basic qualifications are for each different patent-eligible category listed in the statute.

Let's start with the first one:

1 Title 35 U.S. Code § 10 - PATENTABILITY OF INVENTIONS

1. **Process.** What is a process? When you think about it, many common milestones in life are a process: getting a high school diploma or buying a house, for example, are certainly processes.

   Let's break that down a little bit, though. The examples above represent a "set or series of acts" in a certain order and sequence. That's what really makes up a process—a starting point and an ending point.

   Federal law puts it like this: "a process is a mode of treatment of certain materials to produce a given result. It is an act, or a series of acts, performed upon the subject matter to be transformed and reduced to a different state or thing[2]"
2. **Machine.** We talked about the process. Now we will take a look at the patent qualifications for an actual machine. The main difference between a qualifying machine and a qualifying process is that a machine is the sum of various physical parts that carry out a process. If, as we said before, the process is the recipe, the machine is the oven. It is a concrete, empirical object. It consists of parts of certain devices, and there's a combination of devices. Each device, say, a blender, is made of sub-parts. A machine may be made of sub-parts, which need to be fully described. I think this category is probably the most straightforward of the four.

2 35 U.S. Code §10 - PATENTABILITY OF INVENTIONS

We've covered process and machine, let's go to the third type of eligibility.

3. **Manufacture.** When I first started studying patent law, I found this category to be the most abstract of the four—mainly because it sounded (to me) like a work that wasn't quite yet complete.

   The "manufacture" patent designation refers to an article produced from raw or prepared materials by giving to these materials, whether by hand labor, or by machinery, new forms, qualities, properties, or combinations.

   This designation is all about raw materials. Think: wood, water, dirt, chemical compounds and basic, simple mixtures that can be made into more complicated things. This type of patent allows innovators to produce unique products from base ingredients. Much like the process, a patented or eligible manufacture must change the properties of the materials used in regards to their form: the way it actually looks and appears and the shape it holds—in essence, any physical properties.

   Let's say a researcher prepares elements for a study on producing new types of materials for retail packaging. As an initial experiment, he will mix a polymer and a silica with a dioxin, thus transforming plastic and quartz into a bouncy, putty-like consistency.

This is the definition of a change in property: when the R & D technician combined the two materials, they produced a third with unique physical properties. That result defines a manufacture.

Note: The WAY that the raw materials are combined is left open-ended, unless a separate process claim is written.

4. **Composition of Matter.** Let's read the statute definition here:

   All compositions of two or more substances and all composite articles, whether they be the results of chemical union or a mechanical mixture, or whether they be gases, fluids, powders, or solids, for example.

   Though perhaps not obvious at first glance, there is a big difference between the composition of matter and a manufacture. Manufacture is simply combining raw materials and giving them new qualities or properties. Composition of matter, instead, combines and mixes one or more substances such that they form a chemical union, binding their electrons and transforming at the atomic level.

CHAPTER 4

Are Ideas Patentable?

For some reason, many attorneys LOVE to answer this question with a quick, "Absolutely not." Now, technically, they're right–but the spirit of this question really asks: "If I can explain my idea in sufficient detail so that someone like me could make it and use it, can I protect it?"

The answer to THAT question is a resounding "Yes!" Once the inventor is able to articulate with words and drawings in a sufficient amount of detail to enable someone with ordinary skill in the art (POSITA) to make and use the invention, they have just met the requirement for **enablement**.

Here's an example:

> Imagine a classroom full of students at any Technical School in the country. They are learning about a new tool for integrating the Bean programming language with HTML code. To

accomplish this integration, they're using the new TRANS tool.

Their professor presents a flow diagram that describes each step of this process. The students can see how to integrate Bean and HTML one function at a time.

After class, a young student named Smarty, who successfully integrated the two, exclaimed, "I would have never understood that new tool without Professor Wise's flow diagram."

I chose this hypothetical specifically to refer to a recently published patent application for the TRANS tool. The applicant ONLY described functions; namely, the storage function, the retrieval function, and a conversion function, but also addresses other functions, including the HTML result function.

While the applicant did NOT include a flow diagram, it was all laid out in the descriptions of each function from which the Professor was able to create the diagram. In fact, the patent didn't have any detailed schematics or diagrams explaining what order the steps should go in, just the major functions. On top of that, the patent didn't have any code whatsoever. There was actually no Bean programming language in the written description.

Would a patent application similar to the example above still be considered enabling?

Surprisingly, I would say, yes, it definitely seems to be in that category. Remember, you've got to consider that the patent application's audience is not a student, nor even a savvy businessman or woman. Instead, it's the POSITA, the person of ordinary skill in the art. In this case, most likely a computer programmer who would already know that he/she could use many different coding languages to perform the functions. Similarly, a programmer wouldn't need to be instructed on the order of the steps, as they can get the function to work as long as they know how the pieces fit together and what the relationships are.

Remember, in general, no, ideas in and of themselves cannot be patented. One must bring it to life and enable it. In other words, the patent application has to describe a concept in such detail that a POSITA would be able to read it, recognize what's written there and know what the invented steps are in order to be able to innovate again.

CHAPTER 5

THE HEART OF PATENT ELIGIBILITY

Let's begin our discussion of the "heart," or the deciding factor (or factors) in determining the eligibility status of an application by talking about what's NOT eligible—at least since the patent law and the patent clause were inserted into the US Constitution.

NOT ELIGIBLE

Algorithms or pure physical phenomenon, say gravity, or E=MC2, are not protectable. This is mainly because they are laws of nature. Yes, they're complex, and sure, they take a lot of brain power to be understood or applied—but that's not the point here. Laws of nature CANNOT belong to an individual or organization, but to Mother Nature. In other words, they are inherent to the existence of life itself. Our lawmakers made sure to point out that it's not in good faith to potentially allow for someone, an individual, to own something that has been defined by Mother Nature, as opposed to something that has been created by humans.

Now, of course there's lots of arguments going back and forth on that matter, but that's outside the scope of this book.

What's important for our purposes is that the **claims**, or the subject matter regarded by the applicant as the invention eligible for rights of the patent application do, in fact, define the whole of what was invented.

To that end, the language defining the particular scope of exclusivity must be very specific in each application that gets reviewed. Typically, (if working with counsel that's seeking to be an applicant's best advocate) a lawyer will push for the most amount of rights (broadest) as he or she believes possible.

Such claims may start out being quite broad in nature, and as the examiner finds prior art—meaning patents or publications that are similar to the applicant's work, or that may have previously disclosed subject matter to the public that the applicant is trying to claim—some of those broad claims will most likely be limited or amended by the patent office.

In all, if someone asks you what your patent is, it's not really the drawings or the description; it is the claims.

CHAPTER 6

Utility, Novelty, and Non-Obviousness

In reading any patent application, it needs to be apparent to the USPTO how the invention meets (at bare minimum) these three criteria before it will grant a patent. I mentioned these characteristics in earlier discussions on claims. In this Chapter, I will delve into more detail.

Let's take them in order from easiest to most difficult.

Utility, or "immediate usefulness[3]". The eligible invention must have practical benefits in its field or area of technology. Truly, this is one of the lowest bars to be met. In my years of practice, I have not come across any invention that doesn't have at least a shred of usefulness in technology.

Novelty. I use this term a few times in this book, but it's really just a fancy word for "new". The invention must be new; it must have at least one or more inventive

3 35 U.S. Code § 10 - PATENTABILITY OF INVENTIONS

steps beyond the current state of technology in the given field.

Whether the invention is or is not novel enough to be considered for patent rights is confirmed in one of the initial steps we discussed earlier: the **patentability search**. To be sure, the patentability search serves as the supporting evidence in the explanation as to how exactly this invention is part of, or uses technologies beyond the current state.

Obviousness. This last aspect is a little bit trickier to define. We'll spend some time on it.

This requirement states that the innovation must be "nonobvious". The purpose of which is to establish whether or not the invention is trivial. There are two (2) approaches to best determine the individuality of the device or process:

1. **Look for a motivation in the prior art**.
2. **Ask**: **Has the prior art stood up on its own?** Or, could it have been easily combinable with another unit?

Think about obviousness from the perspective of the person of ordinary skill in the art (or post field). Let's say the invention under review is an auto body hammer with a wider than standard head. It could be considered obvious to an auto mechanic, and therefore not eligible for patent rights, that to get more surface area on the hammer, one simply widens the head.

However, the applicant is attempting to claim that since he actually came up with the idea to bend out the rounded edge of the hammer for increased surface area, he should be granted a patent on the design. I think to say that that would have been trivial is an example of a good argument, but it is a case-by-case understanding. If the differences between the proposed invention and the prior art ARE trivial then the invention itself is trivial, and falls into the "too- obvious" category.

Likewise, aside from the small differences, if the entire subject matter of the invention can be shown to be trivial, based on the current knowledge in the industry, the entire <u>subject</u> may be obvious.

What does it mean for an entire subject to be thrown into the proverbial obvious box? Well, for example, an invention regarding a tool for developing software code, would be obvious if some average software developer would have stumbled on it using the known industry knowledgebase. The simple textbook explanation of this is known as: A plus B. In other words, if A is known in the prior art, and B is known in the prior art, assuming that the average software developer knows about A and B, and upon looking at A, and then looking at B, would a POSITA consider A and B together to already be known? If the answer is yes, then A plus B is obvious. If the answer is no, A plus B is not obvious.

CHAPTER 7

Patent Claims and the Tangibility of Digital Products

I've developed a new software app. How does software fit in to the world of patent eligibility?

This is a very good question, and something I get a lot lately. Software developers and, say, groups of engineers collaborate, and oftentimes co-create new software apps. New software apps are coming out thousands, if not tens, or hundreds of thousands at a time. What type of protections should these innovators be seeking? There are two. We'll talk about them each in turn.

- **Patent Protection.** We should talk first about how the scope of patent eligibility for software has become the subject of numerous court decisions just as recently as over the past eighteen months. 2014's Alice Corp vs CLS Bank decision by the Supreme Court has since spurred between 15 and 20 federal court decisions on the subject. These decisions are all over the map, as far as how to try to interpret the Supreme Court's holding, but there has been a basic line of reasoning that the courts have held.

The reason why software recently got this kind of airtime in the courts is because it is a little tricky when it comes to eligibility.

We've discussed the four different types of inventions that qualify for patent rights. The ones easier to define seem to be those things that one can touch and feel: the airplane fuselage that starts out as sheet metal, or as composite material, for example. As it moves through the manufacturing line and goes through additional processes and starts to re-form; as each sheet gets riveted to one another and attached to the frames, soon what was simply a sheet of metal has now become a well-formed position fuselage.

It's not that simple with software, and as one might imagine, there's no big, honking metal parts to see. But if those digital processes have some tangible result and function, they may very well be qualified for exclusivity rights.

As of this writing, it stands in the courts that as long as the claims tie the process steps to a specific machine, the claims could be considered by the USTPO. However, if the "process" is simply a recitation of steps; if an applicant's claim states that "if one were to perform steps

A, B, C, and D, using software on a computer and that these steps should be considered patentable functions performed on the personal computer," there process is too generic.

Unfortunately, that was the case for CLS Bank, as the Supreme Court ultimately said that their financial software application is not patent eligible.

However, this does not mean that there isn't software that IS eligible for protection. As long as the patent claim:

- cites specific problems that the software attempts to solve, and the
- functions can be proven and shown through novel hardware, specific user interface, or specific electrons moving, traveling along a physical line, cable or air-wave, and
- are received by another signal.

THEN you're talking about something that is certainly patent protectable.

Something else to think about in regards to software that many people might not understand is that software is simply a process. The coding belongs more in the domain of copyright.

- **Copyright Protection.** This protection is for the code that developers and/or engineers have produced. Registration for a copyright can be granted through the Library of Congress. Although

I would highly recommend registering software code for a copyright, it is a process that is separate from the patent law, and the USPTO.

SECTION 2

"Obtaining a Patent: The Four Basic Steps"

CHAPTER 8

Step One: Preliminary Patentability Search

After an innovator determines that an idea and/or device includes the subject matter appropriate for patent protection, the first step to obtaining a patent is to perform a Patentability Search. I absolutely recommend having an attorney make a final, expert patentability ruling on any application before it is officially submitted, however, it is extremely useful for the patent-seeker to do their own preliminary search.

What is a Patentability Search? There are general criteria that a design needs to meet in order for it to be considered a work suitable to be granted patent rights. Researching "prior art," or as I discussed in Chapter 5, other works that are similar in type to the patent hopeful's design. In general, "prior art" refers to publicly available information or currently patented claims.

Let's focus on these three (3) categories from Chapter 6:

1. **Novelty.** Is this invention new? Is it too similar to prior art or does the work stand on its own?
2. **Utility.** Is this invention useful? Beneficial in an identifiable way? Although to this day the patent office has yet to disqualify an applicant based on utility alone, it is still a requirement. Furthermore, the courts have recently ruled that the invention must also be "immediately useful[4]" in its art.
3. **Non-Obviousness**. Briefly, this is a metric that measures how well the POSITA chosen to test the considered invention would be familiar with the technology described in the application plus all of the other devices, material and knowledge that's known to those in their industry.

With these criteria in mind, innovators can use any of the many databases available, most through online subscription or registry, and select 5 to 10 prior art examples that MOST SIMILIARLY resemble the work in question to review and compare to their creation. Prior art means inventions, publications, and applications that have already been patented. Now, that these similar methods and/or mechanisms have been previously patented does NOT necessarily mean that the new invention will be denied rights. In many cases, it could simply mean that the

4 35 U.S. Code § 10 - PATENTABILITY OF INVENTIONS

Office will reject some of claims and/or decrease their breadth.

After collecting the cited prior art references from the patentability search, it is now time to get a professional opinion from a registered patent attorney. One should not decide on their own what the preliminary results mean.

An attorney will analyze, compound and summarize the results and give you an opinion on the likelihood of success and scope of what you might be able to get through the patent office. The most valuable part of getting a patentability search and opinion from an attorney, in my opinion, is that it assures the innovator that he or she has done their due diligence to present the best application possible for the sake of their rights as a creator and the potential of their invention.

An attorney can advise on what claims the USPTO may modify and how; or even what rights might be available that the inventor was unaware of, thus streamlining the scope of the product while maximizing its potential in the marketplace.

CHAPTER 9

Step Two: Hire a Registered Patent Attorney

The preliminary patentability results look good.

<u>Great!</u>

Now it is time to HIRE an attorney to vet the completed application. If, at this point, an attorney has not yet been consulted, I repeat, NOW is the time!

Is that really true? In a word: YES.

With a registered patent attorney, the inventor is dealing with an agent that has been registered with the USPTO. This means that this individual has passed a SPECIALIZED patent bar as well as (at least one) state bar. He or she should be an expert in not only patent law, but the laws of the states they practice in.

Keep in mind, attorneys who may understand business law, transactional law, contract law, etc., are good to have on your team of advisers, but are NOT patent agents, are <u>never</u> advisable substitutions.

For instance, a patent attorney has the specialized ability to look at the law from a point of view that understands the trajectory of the USPTO and the federal laws that govern patent infringement. This ability includes unique knowledge regarding trends in order to be proactive when consulting on claim language, drawings, and written specifications.

Should an inventor hire an attorney who is not registered with the USPTO, or if he or she attempts to complete and submit the application without representation, they are taking a HUGE risk with their invention and the power of their claims, and ultimately the potential rights and revenue/profit the exclusivity could bring.

It happens quite often in my practice. Usually, it is the inventor who has decided that in order to save money they draft their own application. I understand that in someone else's opinion; from one who is NOT a patent attorney, writing and submitting one's own application may seem acceptable.

The non-represented inventors may lay out their cases to the best of their abilities. They might very well produce the invention claims, a strong description and/or make beautiful drawings all without consulting an attorney. To be sure, the claims, descriptions and/or drawings that inventors put together as the initial draft of a patent application are crucial. The sad part is that these do-it-yourself inventors may actually get one or more claims through the patent office all the way to grant. The catch is that the claims that are granted are usually not worth the paper they are printed on because they do not adequately cover the invention, or are so narrow that future innovators can easily design around them to compete in the marketplace – thus losing any competitive advantage.

To further emphasize the importance of such a review, I'll bring up the concept of **enablement**, or, according to the Manual of Patent Examining Procedure (MPEP), "any analysis of whether a particular claim is supported by the disclosure in an application requires a determination of whether that disclosure, when filed, contained sufficient information regarding the subject matter of the claims as to enable one skilled in the pertinent art to make and use the claimed invention."[5]

It hurts (usually) when I have to tell an inventor that they have not enabled all the areas in which they wish to claim. In developing perhaps only one aspect of their invention and not elaborating or thoroughly defining the invention in its entirety, one will almost certainly drastically limit their outlook and the potential claims that may exist for them.

It can be a tough conversation. Usually, I approach the client with a solution that focuses on expanding the breadth and nature of the claims.

I explain that there IS a risk that someone else in their field beat them to the patent office in the time since filing their own. However, I also explain to them that it is certainly worthwhile to review and edit those areas that they did not describe thoroughly. Some inventions

5 Chapter 2100. Section 2164: 2164.01 Test of Enablement [R-08.2012]

that are indeed different but happen to be similar in nature or subject matter may appear to be the same. It is therefore imperative that the application—especially the claims—illustrate the distinctive properties and functions of an invention as clearly as possible.

This means that there will be a second round of examinations and that we (the client and I) need to prepare. The inventor's job is to update the application to reflect the changes and feedback from the USPTO. The attorney's job is to analyze and give the inventor an expert opinion on that feedback, for the most part, in terms of what rights to focus on obtaining.

So not to worry! This back and forth is pretty standard. But there is one thing...

For clarity's sake, I then broach the obvious: this also means more time. Maybe a lot more. And more professional work hours[6].

It is, however, part of the purpose of this book to inform prospective applicants BEFORE they make any formal commitments or submissions. In this way, I aim to get people familiar with the process in the hopes of saving future applicants from (at least any further) frustration and/or discouragement.

In any event, when embarking on the patent process, I highly recommend that every creator work with a registered patent attorney. As I mentioned, the patent laws change frequently. We saw some of the reasons for this when we discussed the state of software patents in Chapter 7. As I said, this change in software that I

6 See Chapter 10 for details

described happened within the past eighteen months, since the summer of 2014 and the decision of Alice[7]. All subsequent decisions happened within months, if not weeks, prior to the transcription of this book. Though I have said it before, I'll say it again very clearly: Do not file an application through the USPTO alone. This invention could be extremely valuable. It could change the world. Do it right: make sure it is properly protected.

7 Alice Corp. v. CLS Bank

CHAPTER 10

Step Three: Estimate Application Costs

How much does it cost to file a patent?

Such a simple question, but also a smart one to ask up front, as the answers are many and varied. Relatively speaking, the cost of a patent from start to finish is a considerable amount of money. The following is a list of what the expense covers. It is a helpful tool for any innovator looking to take the next steps with a professed new invention.

- **Professional Work Hours.** The true, first up-front cost is the time and effort it takes the inventor to do their preliminary patentability search before approaching an attorney. This is a cost that's not normally calculated, but I think it is no less valid.

Is it worth the time?

A better question to ask one's self would be: How much work should you do when you have an invention or an idea that you think deserves patenting?

In most cases, one will want to do some personal leg-work to make sure the design is, by and large, something new. I highly recommend doing AT LEAST a Google or a Bing search for criteria and resources of information about prior art[8].

Attorney's Fees. As per the steps listed in this book, once the initial diligence is done it is time to approach a patent attorney. These costs can, of course, be broken down as well.

Initial Consultation. It would be my guess that at this point, the patent expectorant has spent about an hour or so discussing the invention with his or her attorney. As of this writing, that average cost is somewhere around $300.

At this point, based on the information obtained from an attorney, it will be clear whether or not the subject matter at hand is at present patent-eligible or whether

8 Remember the requirements we discussed in Chapter 6?

1. Novelty
2. Utility
3. Non-obviousness

Use these categories as guidelines for your research.
As a suggestion, study causes and different types of reactions that come from your chemical invention, if that's what you've done. Or, how about different sub-devices and effects and functions of the new apparatus that you've just created? These are perfect things to be searching for.

the attorney recommends a more informed, thorough and objectively done patentability search.

Patentability Search by Attorney reg. w/ the USTPO. In my experience, I recommend a patentability search be conducted to about 80% of my clients. The search, focused mainly on the novelty requirement to answer once and for all: is this invention new? Is it a step beyond where the current state of the art is now?

The USPTO examiners do their own searching once the application is submitted. Because of this, there are a handful of attorneys who might say that a patentability search is not worth the time, since the examiners will perform their own anyhow.

Then why the need to do a search up front? Why try to anticipate what the examiner is going to find?

My answer to this is simply one of economics. As I said, there is a considerable cost for the inventor or the business owner in getting the application completed and ready for submittal to the USPTO. Before the inventor were to invest in furthering the process, i.e. draft an application, pay an attorney for counsel, strategy, filings, etc. he or she would be wise to be filled with confidence that this invention is (at least presumptively) new.

Let's look at the process step by step. This will give inventors a better idea of how to scale the costs for their own inquiry.

Drafting the Application. If the inventor or business owner has not done a lot of testing on their invention, or maybe there's no prototype yet and it is still somewhat of a straw horse, it can acceptably be written down and described in an application. However, it is highly recommended that such an application be submitted as what is called a **provisional application**. I recommend this type of application to inventors whose invention has not yet been created, i.e. no prototype. The reason for this is simply that if the concept has not yet been built out, it has not yet been tested, and is therefore likely to change once tests are conducted. In this case, it is virtually impossible to draft solid claims. A provisional application is a less formal version of registering an invention with the USPTO. It does not require explicit claims, the critical component of the (non-provisional) patent application.

At any rate, should the provisional be filed, the applicant can expect the typical fees on a provisional to range from between $3,000 to $5,000, depending on the level of technical complexity.

For example, a simple mechanical application, let's say a stapler, may be even less than $3,000 to put together for a provisional, but a software application with its complexities could easily be $5,000 or more to properly articulate. As we'll discuss later, the fee scale is based on the anticipated time and effort it will take to describe and enable someone that is of the same art as the inventor to build and test the considered invention.

This objective individual is our friend, POSITA. I've mentioned this acronym before and we will continue talking about this objective tester throughout this book.

The POSITA is this reference point that must be considered when drafting a description of what the patent application actually is. I'd say what makes around 80% of the cost of a provisional application is the need to describe in such detail that a POSITA would be able to pick up that written description and make and then use that invention.

Let's talk about the second type of application. If things look good after doing the search and there's maybe only one or two prior art examples that could potentially get close to barring the proposed invention from obtaining rights, I would warn the inventor and/or business owner that the application may need to be limited in one or two respects based on that prior art. The next step would be to file a **non-provisional**.

Of course, no matter what, if an inventor first files a provisional they must eventually file a non-provisional in order to solidify and secure their patent protections.

A **non-provisional** application, as I mentioned earlier, requires explicit claims. Although I covered claims pretty thoroughly in earlier chapters, I am going to touch on them one more time here. Claims are between 40% and 50% of the entire effort of a patent application. Even though they may only comprise one, two, or three pages of what might be a fifty-page specification, the effort and care that's put into crafting those claims is considerable; and this craftsmanship is the true art of the patent attorney.

Non-provisional applications also have more formal requirements with regard to structure and filing, including an invention oath (one must furnish a sworn oath that they are the original and true inventor). The patent office also requires the inventor to submit an information disclosure sheet that identifies all reference points, all prior art and, basically, all the knowledge of the industry that the inventor and the attorney discovered while doing their patentability search. That way, the examiners have all the information available to them that the inventor and attorney had at their fingertips when drafting the application. This helps streamline the examination process for the Office and the POSITA.

What about non-provisional costs?

Because it's a more formal registration, the cost is considerably more. At our firm, Bold IP, we charge between $7,000 and $15,000 for drafting a non-provisional from scratch. However, if a provisional application was used, we take the provisional cost and subtract that from the cost of the non-provisional.

For example, let's say a given provisional application cost a total of $3,000 to submit. If that same applicant were instead ready to apply for a non-provisional patent, the cost would increase to somewhere around $8,000.

Now, if the provisional was filed first, a lot of the work from that application will be used to complete the non-provisional. In this scenario, the additional cost to convert from a provisional to non-provisional would be about $5,000.

The costs at this point are now at a total of about $8,000, plus the costs of having a patentability search done and any time and effort spent pre-attorney.

Now, finally, the application is ready for submission to the USPTO.

Submission and Acceptance by USPTO. If the claims were done right, the language should be quite broad and reflect the intent of the inventor to achieve the most exclusivity possible for their work. As a result, this generally means that examiners will respond by requiring the applicant to limit or modify their claim requests. Thus, the examiner will reject the application—and when they reject, the cost is hourly. The cost does depend on the size and complexity of the rejection, but on the whole you can assume between 8 and 15 hours of work. Ballpark, that's about $3,000 per office action.

Even if the application is done exactly right, one can expect maybe two or even three office actions to go back and forth, with the attorney trying to argue on his client's behalf in an effort to get the most possible rights.

Let's say for this hypothetical application the worst case scenario has occurred. The inventor incurred $10,000 in office actions. The cost is now up to $18,000... and that is not the end!

As I mentioned earlier, this is not a small amount of money. Applying for a patent can be a big financial decision.

CHAPTER 11

The Patent Application Checklist

While the essential materials are very much the same, there are some basic differences in what is required between the three major types of patent applications.

Let's break down the **utility** patent first. This patent application is one of prose; it's a narrative written by the inventor, with the help of the patent attorney, about the invention. At the highest level it must be written in such a way that it fully describes the invention, so that a colleague or similar, the examiner we know as the POSITA, a person of ordinary skill in the art, will be able to make it and use it.

A patent application for a **design**, on the other hand, is extremely short, and as you would expect, the focus of that application is on the drawings. There is actually only one claim in a design patent application and the predominant features are described in the figure description. Figure 1, for example is an isometric view. Figure 2 is a side view, figure 3 is a top view and so on.

An application for a **plant** patent very much resembles the utility patent application. The main difference, however, is that the claimant must provide the USPTO with a specimen of the plant.

What else needs to be submitted to the USPTO?
There are (9) **NINE** subsections of the patent application.

1. **Fee transmittal form.** This form, as one might expect, covers the fees that are owed to the USPTO for doing a search and for maintaining the file on an electronic server, as well as doing an examination. Once this form is completed, it must be included along with the rest of the files.
2. **Entity Size.** The second major document is the document that declares the applying entity's size. If it is a solo inventor, and this inventor has not assigned the rights of the invention to a company and has not filed more than 4 patents in their life and makes less than three (3) times the median income, they can file for what's called a **micro-entity**. The USPTO offers substantially reduced fees for these types of inventors.

   The next entity qualification, as mentioned in Chapter 10, **small entity**, exists for the inventor who does make more than three (3) times the median income; or if the inventor is part of a business that has fewer than 500 employees and does not have any assignment of their invention to a company that has more than 500 employees.

The fees are still reduced, just not quite to the degree of a micro-entity.

Of course, there are full fee rates for the entities larger than 500 employees.

3. **Micro-entity.** The third major document is the **micro-entity** as discussed earlier, depends largely on gross income of the applicant(s).
4. **Specification.** This document is one of the most important parts about an application. It contains, as we discussed before, the actual description of the invention in a truly enabled way.
5. **Drawings.** The drawings must make reference to the specification. This means that the most important parts of the drawing are to be labeled numerically, numbers say 1-10 on figure 1. These numerals 1-10 will then refer to a description in the specification particularly regarding their position relative to one another. For example, a flow chart for example. The order in the sequence in the description must follow the same sequence that is in the drawing in the specification.
6. **Claims.** The sixth major document is the **claims**. Claims are the most important part of the patent application. They comprise, legally, what the heart of the patent is—what the inventor claims that is legally theirs by creation or discovery. What about the design is new? What new technology does it use? What does it do? How do these answers fit together to create something commercially viable?

7. **Application Data Sheet.** The application data sheet includes all the information about the inventor. Who they are, where they are from, if they have assigned the invention to an entity and whether they are filing based on a reference or a prior filing. For example, when one files a non-provisional application, they must re-cite the provisional application that was filed before their non-provisional in order to claim priority to the provisional application.
8. **Information Disclosure Sheet** is the IDS, which stands for the Information Disclosure Sheet.

   There are 2 major IDF forms that must be submitted:

> The **first** of which refers to the granted patents that were either reviewed or used as references in the development of the invention and the bounds of the claims.
>
> When the inventor's attorney does the patentability search, all of the patents that turn up as part of that search will go into an IDF, as well as all of the patents that the inventor along the way.
>
> The **second** information disclosure sheet are the **non-patent documents**. These are the publications and/or the internet widgets that are found in non-granted patents. These are also published applications of pending patents that are

before the USPTO. All of those materials must be cited in the IDF.

9. **The Inventor's Oath**. Also called the declaration. Inventors must give a signed oath, declaring that they believe themselves to be the true inventor of the device, apparatus, method, whatever it is they are claiming is patentable. This is submitted with the entire package.

All of these documents together comprise the whole of the patent application. Each document must be submitted in the right time, and in the right manner so that the USPTO can receive them according to their specific requirements.

For the most part, this consists of having an attorney upload each file as a PDF into the electronic system at the USPTO.

CHAPTER 12

Step Five: Examiner Review

So I finally got my application submitted. How long until the USPTO responds?

To be sure, the length of time before the Office reaches an initial decision varies considerably. Yes, I know this is a very lawyerly type of answer, but based on the variety and complexity of applicant designs, it most certainly does depend.

What are the major factors that determine how long it will take for the USPTO to respond?

Technology area. Within the USPTO there are hundreds of different art units. These art units are comprised of half a dozen or more examiners and one senior examiner. Each examiner works in one specific area only. For example, this could be semi-conductors, or lawn equipment or maybe even home furnishings! You name the type of technology and there is an art unit assigned to review applications related to it.

That said, the USPTO tends to lag in its general turnaround time.

What do I mean by that?

Well, the art units tend to be understaffed in comparison to demand. This is a function of the ebb and flow of culture and commerce.

Take software applications, for example. Ten or fifteen years ago software apps were nowhere near as numerous as they are today. This unit was quite possibly overstaffed a decade ago, but is now badly understaffed.

In other words, the Office cannot necessarily anticipate trends in innovation in terms of what art units to beef up and which ones to slim down quickly enough to accommodate optimal expedience.

The Market. As a natural extension of cultural and technological shifts and the consequent art unit staffing issues, the second reason for any delays in processing is the market itself.

When I use the term "market" I am referring to the number of applications in the pipeline for each art unit and how overloaded or behind those units are.

With this inevitable lag in mind, I tell my clients to generally expect to wait between three to four years for their patent to be granted. I give them this extended timeline to give the client the worst case, most conservative answer to temper expectations. Of course, my goal is to get the patent granted sooner.

Luckily, there are a couple of different strategies on how to do just that.

How does this time lag affect the process as a whole? Before I describe these strategies, it is important that one be aware that during this lag—while his or her patent is pending—the design DOES NOT hold any enforceable rights. Because of this, the invention itself, as well as the innovator's stake or potential stakes, can be at risk.

For instance, someone has filed a patent for a new type of floor jack that is designed to make lifting a car much easier.

To digress for the sake of this example, mechanics have always had issues with using the standard single jack underneath one tire. Now, an automotive engineer or experienced mechanic has devised a way to where the user will be able to have one jack that can jack up BOTH the left and right front tires to gain access to the engine underneath.

Once a patent application has been filed with the USPTO, regardless of how long ago it was submitted, if someone else comes up with the same idea and begins selling it commercially (assuming of course they've come up with the idea on their own) there's no way you can stop them from doing so. A pending design is NOT protected!

As an agent of the USPTO, I can tell you that the Office DOES understand that these problems arise and are doing their best to resolve any dispute of claims by making prosecution as speedy as possible[9].

Realistically, odds are no one is going to be independently inventing and selling the submitted idea. Also, if and when the patent application does get to grant, the filer, in some cases, has the ability to enforce their rights retroactively. However, one is required to prove that the infringing party knew that there was a pending application and willfully infringed.

That said, let's now talk about a few of the petitions one might file in an effort to mitigate that three to four year delay.

Age Waiver. One way to speed up the process is to petition for an age waiver. This means that if over the age of 65, an inventor can apply for a petition to get to the front of the line.

Obviously, this method has very strict eligibility criteria. The USPTO offers this type of waiver because of their missive to make sure that the inventor is indeed

---

9 The USPTO offers the ability to make your application "special" by paying for an expedited fee (which guarantees an office action within 1 year) and is a good option for those applications which are potentially being infringed while in the application stage (before rights have been granted)

Note, pre-grant protection is available under 35 U.S.C. § 154(d), which allows a patent owner to obtain reasonable royalty damages for certain infringing activities that occurred before patent's date of issuance. This right to obtain provisional damages requires a patent holder to show that (1) the infringing activities occurred after the publication of the patent application, (2) the patented claims are substantially identical to the claims in the published application, and (3) the infringer had "actual notice" of the published patent application.

rewarded for their invention. Thus, this is one of my favorite petitions.

In most cases, those over the age of 65 that have properly filed the petition for the waiver, can expect to get an action within one year and potentially granted their patent within two years—as much as twice as fast.

1. **Accelerated Examination.** Another way to expedite an action and grant is to pay for it. The Office will conduct a special search of the application, called an accelerated examination, to see if it meets their requirements. This search costs upwards of $2,000 to $3,000—however, one can expect to get an action within a year.

   There are other grounds on which to apply for an accelerated examination, although these types of petitions are outside the scope of this book. I will, however, cover one more.
2. **Critical Technology.** The USPTO rewards those inventions that try to solve problems in the environmental arena. If the patent and the claims are construed to be new environmental technology, specifically in the area of environmental progress, i.e. improving the air quality, referencing climate change and energy, etc. Pending inventions that pose solutions to these types of issues are put to the front of the line.

CHAPTER 13

STEP SIX: APPLICATION MAINTENANCE

The application has completed the examination phase! Now an **issue fee** is due and the **maintenance fees** begin.

Maintenance fees are due at three and a half, seven and a half and eleven and a half years. Also, these fees rise in proportion to the size of the entity that owns the patent.

As with all USPTO fees[10], beginning even at the application[11] level, the cost depends on how big of an entity it is that is filing.

a) <u>Micro-entity</u>. The average individual inventor that does not make more than three (3) times the national median income is considered a

10 See "Basic Filing Fees" at http://www.uspto.gov/learning-and-resources/fees-and-payment/uspto-fee-schedule

11 Maintenance fees are also proportional.

micro-entity and will pay a far reduced payment of $70 for a provisional application.

b) Small Entity. If that individual were to make three (3) times or more the median income, then they are a small-entity and would pay a proportionate $120 to the micro-entity fee of $70.

c) Regular Entity. A regular entity has 500 or more employees and is an un-discounted entity. Their cost for the same hypothetical filing would be around $200.

Let's get back to our overall calculations. We were at roughly $18,000 for the cost of a non-provisional patent application. Let's assume that this applicant is a small entity. To be conservative, the total maintenance fees would be around $6,000 for the life of the patent:

- **3 1/2** years it would be $800
- **7 1/2** years it would be $1,800
- **11 1/2** years it would be $3,700

That's a total of just under $7,000 for that time period for maintenance fees.

In all, the cost is now estimated to be $18,000 plus $7,000, or about $25,000. That's minimum. It assumes no **continuations** or **continuation-in-part**, no appeals or the like.

SECTION 3

"How It Works: Rights and Infringement"

CHAPTER 14

Provisional vs. Non-Provisional Applications

Essentially, the purpose of a provisional application is to provide the inventor with a patent pending status for their creation. A non-provisional does the same thing, but requires a lot more formal language, structure, clear-cut and detailed claims, as well as very specific drawing requirements.

As previously mentioned, a provisional application is much less formal. The language does need to be written down very carefully (see "enablement" as discussed before) but it does NOT require claims, nor does it require specific drawings, headings and certain other criteria within the specification, including the inventor's oath. This obviously makes the initial application process easier for both the inventor and the attorney.

One of the other main differences is the order in which to file each one. Because of this, I will go over the timeline once more:

- File **Provisional Application**.
- Third Party Introduction (as needed)
- **Acceptance** by USPTO
- **Start 1 Year Deadline** to Submit Full, **Non-Provisional Application**
- Testing, Build-Out, Creation of Full Claims, Description, etc. for **Non-Provisional Application**
- **File Non-Provisional**

During this one-year time period, a lot of the functions and a lot of the main aspects of the invention will evolve and the specification therefore will need to be rewritten. Remember, this evolution is, of course, because the claims, the core reason for which IP protection exists, have not yet been written[12].

What really needs to be written down?

The keyword here is **enablement**. That sure sounds like a vague and complex legal word—and it can be. Still, in the patent lingo it's one of the most important words to know. To satisfy the requirements of a provisional application, one must, via written description, enable the POSITA to understand how to build out and use the invention. In the vernacular, the provisional application has to be enabled: it must be described all the way down to the nuts and bolts.

12 They will be outlined as required and included in the non-provisional application. The reason claims need to have very specific, careful attention paid to them is so that they draw the broadest possible invention from the specification. Every word counts when it comes to the claims.

Let's sum up the differences:

As I said before, it is also a lot less formal than the non-provisional. Any drawings do not need to have the numerals labeled. They don't need to necessarily have a proper order, size or image. They simply need to create a basis so that the non-provisional application can claim priority.

Along with the level of work required for each—obviously the provisional requiring less work and the non-provisional requiring more work—comes a respective price difference between what it costs for an attorney to complete each one. Don't forget the cost and time for the inventor as well. If an inventor is currently preparing to do a non-provisional that usually means that they have already done a lot of the prototyping and testing. Most likely, the invention would not change much in the next six months.

Filing a provisional makes sense if a prototype has not yet been created, or if there is a prototype, it hasn't really been tweaked to a version of the model and the product or service has not yet sold anything or been put on the market.

CHAPTER 15

THE THREE MAJOR PATENT TYPES

There are three major types of patents available. They cover three major categories of intellectual property (IP):

1. **Utility.** This patent type protects the structure, operation, or composition of a machine, product or process. The protection essentially covers the function of the innovation. When you hear utility patent, think, what does it do? That is one of the assets that is eligible for protection.
2. **Design.** A design patent protects the non-functional aspect. The fancy word for this type of asset is an "ornamental feature."

   The first thing that comes to mind when I hear the word "ornamental" is Christmas. And, yes, just as Christmas ornaments are aesthetically valuable, the term "ornamental" in this context also refers to a distinctive design, or physical appearance. The design patent covers an exact image. The bounds, the means, the way the image is shaped, the size, and all of the different features that comprise the image's precise characteristics can be protected under a design patent.

3. **Plant.** A plant patent, is awarded to someone who has invented or discovered an asexually reproduced variety of plant. This means that the new strain is fully reproducible in a lab setting without having to rely on mother nature/ pollination.

   For instance, there is a popular strain of apple called the Fuji. The Fuji tree has both a male and a female seed. To reproduce, it requires pollination from bees or birds or from Mother Nature, one may say, to actually take the pollen from the male plant and bring it to the female so that it can bear flowers and apples. Therefore, a Fuji tree would not qualify for a plant patent.

   Remember, to obtain a plant patent, the new strain under examination must have been invented or discovered. Plant patents can be discovered and therefore patented even if the inventor didn't actually breed and grow it themselves. If someone comes across a new species or variety of plant that qualifies, they can apply for a plant patent and claim the flora as their own to use.

TYPE SUBSETS

In this Chapter, I will review these subsets as well as go into more detail on each one of these three aspects.

Utility Subsets. There are some subsets of inventions within a utility patent. They're issued for the invention of a new and useful:

1. Process
2. Machine
3. Manufacture
4. Composition of matter;

or a new and useful improvement thereof. Let's take a closer look at each one.

Process. If you have invented a "use process" or "step by step" process and each of the steps in the process meets the USTPO requirements for IP[13]; if the process is new, if each of those steps in that particular sequence is non-obvious, and if its functionality has real-world, real-time usefulness in the art, then yes, that process would be eligible to be considered for a utility patent.

Machine. The machine claim is defined as just that: a systematic combination of components or sub-devices that comprises a larger machine.

Manufacture. The manufacture is a combination of raw materials. Think of a desk. A wooden desk is comprised of both polymers and the raw material of wood. Often times you've got rubber grommets, certain sealants,

13 Recall from previous chapters, it must be new, novel, non-obvious, and must have utility.

and a polyurethane coat. I'm not saying that's new, but that's an example of a manufacture. It's a combination of raw materials in a specific manner.

Composition of matter. This one comes up most often in the chemical arts, when inventors are dealing with materials such as hydrogen, water, carbon, etc. Material combinations at the molecular and nuclear level, or perhaps different quantities of those molecules in different varieties at certain temperatures or pressures, for example, may be eligible for a patent under this utility subset.

All four of the utility subsets, along with any useful improvements of them are covered under what is called the utility patent. Approximately 90% of the patent documents issued by the USPTO are utility patents.

Design Subsets. These are for new, original, and ornamental designs that are embodied in, or applied to, an article of manufacture. Let's stop right there. Design patents don't cover just anything. The design candidate can't be some imaginary object. It has to be manufacturable. Plainly, the design must have some industry component. The application would have to show that the design is an integral part of a manufacturable physical object or a symbol, let's say a necklace design or a moon-shaped paperweight. Designs for jewelry or physical representations of symbols that are reducible to actual manufacture are candidates for this type of patent.

Under the auspices of a design patent, the owner is permitted, for a designated period, to exclude others from making, using, or selling their particular design just like an invention under a utility patent. What's different about design patents from utility, plant, and other patents, is that the design patent is only good for **14 years** from the date of patent granting. Now with a utility patent, the invention is good for 20 years from the date of patent application filing. It could be said that the utility patent allows for a longer life, but not in all cases. For example, if it were to take up to 6 years to get the non-provisional utility application to the patent office (a rare but very possible event), the two would then have the same life after issuance.

Plant Subsets. Issued for a new and distinct, invented or discovered asexually reproduced plants. As I said before, different types of plants such as spores, mutants, hybrids, and newly found seedlings can be patented under a plant patent. There is one type of plant species, however, that is not eligible. They're called tuber propagated plants. These plants are like the artichoke, or a potato and they've been ruled out because this group alone, among asexually reproduced plants, is propagated by the same part of the plant that is sold as food.

The Utility, Design and Plant patents comprise the three major categories of protection awarded by the USPTO.

CHAPTER 16

PATENT EXPIRATION DATES

Let's go over the lifespan of a patent in detail:

Expiration: Utility. This patent expires 20 years after the filing date. To be specific here, this is <u>not</u> counted from the provisional filing date, but the **non-provisional** filing date. I know it's a little shocking, but it may take up to two to three years to get through the patent office. When this happens, that time is not given back to the inventor. However, there are certain allowances, under certain circumstances that make the application eligible for a **patent term extension**.

If the delay is caused by the patent office, which can be a common occurrence, they will grant the inventor a patent term extension. Most often, the USPTO gets overloaded and behind schedule. When this happens, once the patent is officially granted, they give the inventor time back on the life of the patent.

However, it is true that any time spent in prosecution over the lifetime of the patent—at least a year and a half to two years—is not going to be extended. Potentially, the inventor can expect the patent to have 17 to 18 years of life after being granted.

Expiration: Design application. Regardless of how long it takes in the patent office, going back and forth, whether the design is novel or non-obvious, the design is given 14 years after issuance.

CHAPTER 17

Foreign Patent Rights

Any initial foreign filing MUST be completed within twelve months of any prior U.S patent application from which the claimant would like the benefit of the same filing date.

More simply put, the twelve months starts from the U.S. application date. Now, this does not just reach back to the non-provisional date, this reaches back to the provisional date. If a provisional was filed, let's say in March 2016, which means that by March 2017 the inventor must file an international patent application to claim the benefits of the provisional that was filed back in March 2016.

This works the same way with a non-provisional. If a non-provisional application was filed in March 2016, by March 2017, within twelve months, is the longest time period possible to make reference back to that earlier March 2016 date. Still, if this same application was filed as a provisional before being filed as a non-provisional that international application could not make the claim of benefit to anything earlier than March 2016. In most countries, the initial filing is accomplished with a single international application, called patent cooperation treaty (or PCT) application.

International protection from the PCT serves primarily to preserve an inventor's filing right in countries that have signed this cooperation treaty, but also provides a preliminary examination that can be used to address any issues that relate to patentability prior to filing in any of the individual countries.

This means that if, sticking with the above application example, a PCT application is filed BEFORE March 2017 that makes reference to that March 2016 original filing date. Filing by March 2017 allows the inventor to (with PCT countries) claim priority internationally all the way back to a U.S filing in March 2016.

The PCT application preserves the right to enter into the marketplaces of commercially viable international countries such as Germany, France, Korea and Japan, to name a few. Many different countries require that inventors file within a twelve month deadline in the same sense that the United States requires for a non-provisional from a provisional.

In effect, the PCT gives the inventor more time to think about which individual countries they'd like to file in. If he or she wishes to obtain patent protection in countries that have not signed the PCT, such as Taiwan, they must file applications directly with the patent officers of those countries, usually within twelve months from their U.S filing date.

Then, patent-seekers must file national applications in their chosen countries **30 months** after the original U.S filing date. That gives the applicant another 18 months after filing with the PCT to submit an application in the foreign country of their choosing.[14]

In addition to the expense of submitting an application in the U.S., filing for foreign patent protection is relatively quite expensive. That said, one should hardly base their decision to file or not on anything related to international eligibility.

In my experience, most individuals or entities with limited resources are probably better off spending funds and work hours on marketing, sales, and commercializing the invention than on international patent rights. For the most part, filers choose to extend their rights beyond the American market to a specific country for a specific reason. One easy way to explain this is that many countries are home to different cultures, of course, which means different marketplaces with different demands for certain products. Therefore, some patents have more immediate usefulness in a particular geographic location and lend themselves to qualifying specifically for patent rights in countries outside the U.S.

14 Applications in the European patent office can be filed 31 months after your original U.S filing date, so they allow one more extra month.

CHAPTER 18

Monetize Your Patent

There are a number of ways to make money from a patent—even before it's granted. In fact, one of the first things I do with new clients is sit down with them and help them draw up a business plan.

My goal is to help enable them to use the patent process as a back bone; a leverage point to launch a business. Of course, that business can take many shapes, and as I teach them the different options for how to monetize their patent, I remind my client that, as the inventor, it is important that they consider the different ways and avenues in which they might be able to achieve success using their innovation and its patent rights.

These options are:

1. **In-House.** One of the first and most traditional ways to monetize a patent is to keep it in-house. Step one is to set up a business entity with an appropriate state.

Perhaps an inventor wishes to establish a sole proprietorship or regular LLC to monetize her mechanical device. She would then begin manufacturing the devices and selling them, either locally or internationally through the web, or both.

While this might seem like the traditional format, it is actually becoming less and less the case that the inventors themselves want to take up the concomitant responsibilities of commercially producing, marketing and selling their device.

2. **License the Rights.** The second option for an inventor is to license the rights to their granted patent. There are three main rights that make up the traditional set of patent grants and they are:
   - the right to make,
   - the right to use, and
   - the right to sell.

   There are other, more specialized rights, such as the right to offer for sale, export into other countries, but for our purposes let's keep it simple and stick to those three: to make, use, and sell.

   What that means, in terms of how licensing works, is that the inventor can assign and allow a third party to make, use or sell (or a combination of them) for a profit.

   The inventor of the mechanical device from our example could create an agreement with a manufacturer in Florida that has a client, a retail company in San Diego who is looking to sell a product just like hers. For a fee, the inventor would create a licensing agreement with the company in Florida to make her device so that they can sell it to the retail company.

To that end, it is important for inventors to be aware that they can choose to make such agreements either exclusive or non-exclusive.

Under a different licensing agreement, this inventor could agree with the company in Florida to make that same arrangement a non-exclusive license. As with any contract structure, there are pros and cons as well as more prudent times to offer either exclusive or non-exclusive licensing deals.

First off, if the license is non-exclusive, the manufacturer is not going to be willing to pay out as much money. The reason for this is simple: if the inventor also sells the license to a different manufacturer in Charleston, South Carolina, they, too could go into business producing the device and sell them to the same retailer in San Diego. All of a sudden there's a lot more competition. What this allows the inventor to do is potentially license to more than one manufacturer. While each contract pays out less, the patent owner does not have all her eggs in one basket.

Think about all the different licensing avenues (read revenue streams) that could come from this: different manufacturers, different users, and different sellers potentially worldwide.

3. **Sell the Patent Rights.** The third option is to simply sell the patent outright. The inventor may sell the rights of the patent and be reimbursed for their innovation and contribution to society.

   What's important to note about a sale is that the inventor needs to make sure that they have representation and a formal evaluation done on their patent and what it could really bring in the marketplace. Once this has been done and a fair offer's been made by a party, a sale can then be transacted. Remember, one of the key variables in a patent valuation is that the market value depends on the scope of the claims. It also heavily depends on the geographical locations where the patent application has been filed. The patent can have rights in the States, but it may also have rights in Europe or Asia and the Middle East. Where and how many places the patent holds rights also affects the price tag.

CHAPTER 19

THE BASICS OF ENFORCEMENT

Does patent protection guarantee that my innovation will be safe from infringement?

Unfortunately no. Since it's not a crime to infringe a patent in the US, there is no government agency or prosecutor that will go after those dirty infringers. This is the sole responsibility of the patent owner. No one is going to help enforce the rights of the inventor or entity and the patent right therein.

This is why most patent holders hire a patent attorney to perform infringement analysis. They want to keep tabs on the marketplace and any possible infringement upon the claims of their patent right.

To begin this analysis, one of the first steps the patent attorney will do is a thorough examination and analysis of the claims. As I have repeated, the claims of the patent are its heart. This analysis will look at the claims of your patent and then carefully at the accused infringer's activities. Whether product or service, each or any of those commercially sold items that the alleged infringer is offering, will be analyzed against the claims. If in fact the claims are being infringed upon, the patent attorney will issue notice letters or cease-and-desist letters regarding certain activities in the market place.

Having to file a lawsuit in federal court to stop an infringer is the worst case scenario and last resort. The first step to taking down an infringer is a notice or cease-and-desist letter. These letters describe in very specific detail what parts of the infringing body's activities are actionable. The more specific, the better. If the infringer sees that the patent holder has done their homework, that their attorney has been scrutinizing each of their activities and highlights precisely which claim and what language is being infringed on, more often than not the infringing party will comply and cease their activities. Usually responding with something like, "Oh, I'm sorry. I didn't realize it."

Next, they will likely either shut that part of their business down or to come to the negotiating table with the inventor and negotiate terms to license the rights. It can be a winning situation to settle for both parties. The inventor gets awarded for their invention, and to the infringer gets to continue being in business—assuming that they can afford to pay the royalties and the license fee ALONG with making a profit.

On the other hand and as I alluded to earlier however, the dispute may come down to a court case. This is rare, but infringers sometimes decide to deny their wrongdoing outright and say, "Oh no, I'm not infringing on that patent."

Dealing with these sorts of cases requires a lot more effort. Although patent litigation is outside the scope of this book, it is very important to retain patent counsel in the event of any litigation.

CHAPTER 20

Infringement and Intent

It does not matter if a party intended to infringe or if they were altogether unaware that the patent existed. They are infringers both, just as liable under the civil rule: whoever without authority makes, uses, offers to sell, or sells any patented invention within the United States or imports it into the United States infringes the patent. That's the law and it's pretty clear: there is no intent requirement.

Still, this is not to say that intent NEVER matters. For that reason, I'm going to dig into the law just a little bit more here.

There are more than just the direct infringers. There are what's called **contributory infringers**. Contributory infringement arises when a company, well, contributes toward the infringement. For instance, a widget that is being produced has a handle and a spinning top. The manufacturer makes the handle, but not the top. They only make a mold for the spinning top. It is the job of another manufacturer to make the top itself and then connect it to the handle.

The second manufacturer is a direct infringer. The first manufacturer is a contributory infringer. They haven't made the top per se, but they DID enable another entity to manufacture it. It's still infringement, just not in a clear, direct way. Therefore, in these cases, the courts have said that in order to be liable for infringement, the accused must have intended on it. In other words, the contributor must have had a certain amount of knowledge of the patent to be found liable.

In the case of the top mold manufacturer from the example, it could very well be that before they gave that mold and handle to the second manufacturer they knew that there was a patent on the part. It's almost at issue why wouldn't they just make the top. Were they were trying to be smart about it? Perhaps they were trying to avoid liability by simply making the mold for the top. That's exactly what this law was intended to prevent: those who exploit loopholes and skirt the law.

Another case in which intent is a factor in liability is known as willful infringement. A party is willfully infringing when they have been put on notice by the patent owner, yet have not stopped their infringing activities. Now, going back a chapter or two, when a patent attorney, on the inventor's behalf, gives a notice or provides a cease-and-desist letter that essentially says, "Hey, you infringer, you should stop selling that widget because we have a patent on it," and if that party reads that letter and says, "Whatever," and sells anyway and doesn't stop at all—they are willfully infringing.

This is important because, according to the law, if willfulness can be proved to the court, then the infringing party will also owe treble damages. No, not trouble, even though that word is also very fitting. Treble is the word. It can mean double or three times the amount of damages that would be awarded under a direct infringement. What's more is that they also have to pay the attorney's fees for the inventor.

CHAPTER 21

WHY CEASE-AND-DESIST LETTERS MATTER

The number one reason to send a notice or cease-and-desist is for the patent owner to establish that they will enforce their patent rights. Number two, it is the space in which to lay out all of the different aspects of the alleged infringement. The patent attorney will identify ***where*** the infringer was, ***what*** the acts were and all the details of the specific parts that address the claims as I mentioned before. Most importantly, it compares the patented features to the suspect features of the accused's product and identifies all of the ways in which these features are being infringed upon as the inventor believes them to be. These letters are highly fact specific.

Thirdly, it puts the other party on notice. Now as I mentioned before, this is very important with regard to whether the other party becomes a willful infringer. If they are put on notice and it is clear that the patent holder has communicated their case regarding the alleged infringement, the onus is now on the accused to make

BoldPatents.com 800-849-1913 info@boldip.com

their own determination of whether the patent holder has a valid case or not. They'd be wise to go seek their own counsel and see if in fact they are infringing as the owner claims. This is the kind of diligence that might avoid their infringement being willful.

Let's think about why it would be important for the patent owner to send a notice letter. Again, it creates the possibility of a good faith negotiation for a settlement. This opportunity is valuable because, really, no one wants to go to court.

What's important for the recipient of a Notice or Cease-and-Desist letter? For one, they are put on notice of their potential infringement. It could be, as is likely in most cases, that they don't know that they are infringing. Receipt of this type of letter gives the liable party options, including the option to attempt to strike first.

This fact is one potential downside for the sender in that once the recipient gets the notice they then have the option to make the first move in court and seek what is called a **declaratory judgement**. A declaratory judgement is one that looks to obtain a definitive ruling of law that states that there is no infringement. To make matters even worse is that the jurisdiction of declaratory judgments, or DJs, are local to the accused infringer.

Remember that the widget retailer from the contributory infringement example was in San Diego and the manufacturer was over in Florida. If that potential manufacturer is infringing on the patent rights of one in San Diego and has received a notice, that Florida based manufacturing company may bring a declaratory judgement action in, say, Fort Lauderdale—now the plaintiff <u>and</u> the defendant both have to meet in that Fort Lauderdale jurisdiction if they want to argue the DJ action.

CHAPTER 22

Patent Trolls: Problems and Solutions

Well, a patent troll is an individual that is, on average, two to three times larger than a human. Predominantly green or brown in color. They have at least three to four warts on either side of their nose and generally stay out of sight by hunkering down beneath the interstate bridge, slowly eating scroll after scroll of patent documents.

Okay, that was fun. Of course, that's not what a patent troll is. A patent troll is usually a large company that acquires patent rights from inventors or other small companies, and simply waits for someone, or some business, to begin infringing on the patent claim, without actually practicing, or selling any products or services in the area of technology. You might also hear the term **non-practicing entity**, or NPE. NPE and trolls are synonymous. Let's break this down a little bit more.

What this means is that a NPE, or a patent troll, the company that buys a patent from an inventor or from a company that owns and is the assignee of an invention or that a patent inventor assigned to that entity.

They can do that?

Well, there really is no requirement to use the exclusive rights that the patent office awards. In fact, patents are sometimes achieved for defensive purposes to simply prevent anyone (including themselves) from making, using or selling.

Again, as we discussed, a utility patent allows for 20 years after the filing date that are purely for the invention owner. No one else can make, use, or sell products or services that use the patented material in the geographic location defined. What that could also mean is that one could even prevent themselves from making, using, or selling the patented property.

In terms of moving things forward in the economy, many people believe that if one goes through all of the trouble to apply for and receive a patent, it ought to be used. Products should be put out into the market. Things should be sold through the services. However, that's just not the reality.

Congress is currently working on bills to stimulate the process of introducing more of these patented products and processes to the marketplace. There are two in particular, one called the Innovation Action HR9, introduced in February 2015 and the other is a Senate bill 1137 that protects the American Talents and Entrepreneurship

Act, or Patent Act. This bill was introduced in mid-May 2015.

In essence, there are three (3) main proposals on the table for how to change some of this activity.

1. **Fee Shipping**. Under Fee Shipping, any NPE that brings an infringement suit and loses may have to pay its opponent's legal fees. This proposal attempts to address the potential problems associated with the non-practicing entities that simply hold on to a patent or patents and wait (lurk) for someone in a technology field to start making widgets that could be infringing on their patent claims.

   Once they find a potentially actionable situation, these entities hope that the business or individual that is ACTUALLY bringing this particular or similar widget to market is just trying to make a buck and didn't do a patent search before they officially went into business.

   If an NPE discovers a possible opportunity to bring suit and files, they are, at this point, basically taking a gamble. Their case depends on their belief that the defendant is profiting from claims that infringe on the patent troll's claims. If Fee Shipping is enacted, then trolling plaintiffs are wrong, then the NPE would have to pay the opponent's legal fees.
2. **Shell entity**. Currently, if an NPE sets up shell companies with no assets, they're basically judgement-proof if it so happens that they get an unfavorable

ruling on an infringement action. The reason for this has to do with complicated corporate and securities law and how entities are set up. The current proposal before Congress is to allow exceptions to corporate laws to pierce through the shell companies and attach judgments directly to the NPEs themselves.

3. **Demand letters**. Demand letters are another word for noted letter or cease and desist letter. Some of the acts sitting before the House of Representatives and the Senate have put forward provisions that deal with vague or misleading demand letters.

   Many of these NPE's, or trolls, will send out very broad, unspecific notice letters that cover quite a large chunk of technology. These types of demand letters are designed to scare potential infringers. When an NPE's claim set is reviewed, however, it is generally the case that their claims are actually a lot more limited.

   If the proposals in front of Congress regarding patent trolls and vague demand letters are enacted, there would then be certain provisions in place to award damages to the wrongfully accused.

SECTION 4

"Additional Guidance for Potential Applicants"

CHAPTER 23

What is the Difference Between Patent Protection and Trade Secret Protection?

How does one decide which mark to apply for to protect their innovation?

Great question. I'll start my answer with some of the legalese language. A patent provides protection against any use of the claimed subject matter, regardless of how the subject matter is obtained, for a limited period of time. A trade secret, on the other hand, provides protection against the use of wrongfully obtained secrets for as long as the trade secret remains a trade secret. A trade secret only protects against wrongful taking of the secret, not against **independent discovery** of the secret.

Patent. I'll unpack that a little bit and get real here: as I've said, the patent is essentially a deal between the government and the innovator.

Remember, when the inventor is drafting his or her patent application, they are required to disclose the entirety of the invention's purpose, plans on how to build it and very explicit claims about how it can best be of value. Once the application is received by the Office, well, the cat is out of the bag, shall we say.

What I mean by this is that the fate of the inventor's blood, sweat and tears—a truly personal asset—lies with a government office, and that the invention will be built and tested by someone in the inventor's own field. There are many risks inherent in this sort of detailed disclosure. Imagine the possible trepidation of a famous chef who, in order to get a business permit for a new restaurant, had to send his menu, complete with recipes and plating presentation to a government office. Now imagine the person who is to examine the restaurant file is also a chef. His work is completely exposed!

Therefore, the inventor obviously is looking for something in exchange. The trade-off is the twenty year monopoly on the invention, protected by the government. This exchange is the essence of; the main purpose and appeal of the patent.

Trade Secret. Some creators and companies like the idea of keeping that sensitive information in-house only. They want the chance to remain at that competitive edge for longer than twenty years afforded by the patent. The risk with this classification of designation is that of, as I refer back to the legal language I used above, <u>independent discovery</u>.

Let's pretend that there is a company in Seattle that's got the hottest trade secret on how to grow a certain strain of marijuana. In in Portland, Oregon, there is a different company that also grows marijuana. The company in Portland doesn't even know that the company in Seattle with the secret strain exits, however, they have done a lot of research and are testing out new strains. One of these strains just so happens to be the same growth process, the same exact strain, down to the same molecule as the protected trade secret held by the company in Seattle. Though unaware that another grower holds a trade secret on this strain, they too, recognize its desirable properties and begin to sell it.

Through a natural progression of the Portland Company's business practices, the "secret" recipe is no longer a secret. The strain was brought to market by an entity other than the trade secret owner. Unlike a patent owner, a trade secret holder does not retain the right to enforce their propriety. Independent creation is not theft and, while it can be considered unfortunate, it is unenforceable.

In other words, many companies can have the same exact trade secret ingredient. It could actually even be the case that one of the most famous trade secrets, the Coca-Cola recipe, is not a secret at all. It could very well be that RC Cola and Coca-Cola actually have the same recipe. In other words, the trade secret designation has no requirement for novelty.

In any case, the exchange for non-disclosure with a trade secret protection allows for the potential for companies to keep the best possible competitive edge on sensitive recipes or formulae for longer than the twenty years offered by patent protection. The risk is then of a second or third party developing the same product and eliminating the initial creator's competitive advantage.

PATENT CHECKLIST

Below is a quick list of the best reasons to choose a patent over trade secret protection:

- **Strong Protection.** If the strongest possible protection for the design is needed, an inventor might seriously consider the patent. If inventors want the best assurance that they will be equipped to prevent any of their competitors within the state, within the country, or even the globe, from obtaining their assets, the patent is the strongest protection.
- **Simplicity vs. Complexity.** Second on the list of things to consider is the complexity of the innovation. Potentially, how subject is it to being reverse engineered? Just like I was saying in Chapter 1, the Coca-Cola recipe might be tricky (if not impossible) to decipher how it was made just from the end product, but someone could very feasibly reverse engineer a two or three piece mechanical device in a proverbial heartbeat. Even if the creators kept such a device as a trade secret, someone will eventually pull the thing apart and figure

out how to put it back together again—and then it's done. Their secret's out and they've lost that competitive edge.

- **Time Frame.** If the limited duration of protection at twenty years is acceptable to an individual or commercial entity, a patent might also be a good choice in this instance as well. Twenty years may seem like a long time, but for a corporation that could exist many generations, if not over a hundred years, the time limit is an important factor to consider. However, if a company is one that iterates and comes up with new innovations constantly, twenty years may be more practical. To be sure, a small mom and pop shop with one main product may not benefit from the twenty year limit.

TRADE SECRET CRITERIA

Back to the Coca-Cola example from above and the first Chapter of Section 1. It would be impossible to merely look at their end product and determine the precise way the formula was heated or how the carbonation was added. This complexity of formula could very well be why the Coca-Cola Company has held on to their trade secret for nearly ninety years.

Again, if it is the case that the innovation is not easily subject to reverse engineering, and the inventor is willing to accept the risk of independent discovery, filing for trade secret protection may be the best option.

Below are the other main characteristics of a strong trade secret candidate:

- **Independent Value**. In order to actually have an enforceable trade secret, the secret must be immediately valuable not just to the inventor, but to the inventor's competitors. It is the company or individual creator's key proprietary information, rather than, or apart from, general business practices.
- **Internal Proprietary Documentation**. Specific systems to keep the trade secret, well, a secret, must be in place. The filing party must be willing to take steps to identify the trade secrets within their company or entity. This means that the company must make a review of all their documents and the mark the ones considered proprietary. In addition, companies are required to train employees on what information is restricted and how to manage these confidential records and reports. This requirement is an effort to help a trade secret owner maintain their designation.
- **Misappropriation Protection.** Federally enforced under the Lanham Act, **misappropriation,** or the theft of the information contained as a trade secret, can happen in several ways, mainly: physical espionage, breaking and entering or employee theft. Should, without proper permission, an employee share a secret with a third party—whether

in exchange for money not is considered misappropriation.

Though federal law protects trade secrets against misappropriation, how the laws will be enforced and what penalties shall be assigned are determined by state laws and each state incorporates different codifications of this enforcement.

These factors, along with all of the other information in this chapter should be carefully considered with the counsel of a Patent Attorney when making the decision between applying for a patent and seeking trade secret protection.

CHAPTER 24

WHY SHOULD INVENTORS WITH NEW INNOVATIONS CONTACT A PATENT ATTORNEY NOW?

When an inventor comes up with an idea that they believe to be truly commercially valuable, it is imperative that they seek counsel as soon as possible, without disclosing it to any third parties. I answer this question so directly because it is THAT important. What's important about limiting disclosure to third parties is that when that idea gets out to another individual and not held in confidence (as a discussion with an attorney would be) the USPTO deems that disclosure to be the same thing as a disclosure to the public, and it starts a clock.

The USPTO does allow a grace period of one year from when an invention is disclosed to the public for its inventor to file for protection. After that one year, the design is dedicated to the public. That means that the invention is no longer owned by the creator. It is now everyone's. Anyone's. Donated by default and offering no compensation to the inventor.

The purpose of the USPTO granting these intellectual property rights is to incentivize invention and reward creators for their hard work. My job is to help keep this system robust. If a potential applicant has not consulted a professional agent of the office and does not understand the process clearly enough, he or she puts themselves at risk.

Therefore, potential applicants must be aware of their time restraints. This risk created by disclosure, at least in part, is the reason why I always advise inventors and entrepreneurs that if they believe that they have produced a commercially valuable product to approach counsel immediately. A registered patent attorney can provide the inventors of prospective secrets with the best advice on how the protections work, who to contact and research, and what process to follow.

If the secret is disclosed to someone before the inventor has spoken to an attorney, there's always the added risk that the person who learned the secrets of what could or should be pending proprietary information will file with the USPTO before the true creator, in effect beating the actual inventor to the office.

If The Scenario You Just Described DID Happen, Does The Original Inventor Have Any Recourse?

Generally, No. Not since 2013, when the American Invents Act was passed by Congress and signed by President Obama. The Act changed the United States from a first to invent country to a first to file country.

Before 2013, if the original inventor could prove that he was, in fact, the first to *independently* invent the disputed design, he could file what was called an **interference proceeding**. This proceeding gave claimants the chance to prove that they themselves had created the secret first. The party that filed first obtained the secret through a public disclosure and had applied for rights before the true inventor was able to submit his application.

But, those proceedings no longer exist. Today, the United States recognizes only "first to file," meaning the first person that submits the application gets protection on the invention—as long as the secret was independently derived.

There is a new provision called the **derivation proceeding** which allows for an inventor to argue that the person who "won the race" to the USPTO actually got the invention idea from them and for lack of a better word, derived or *stole* the idea from the inventor – they can be awarded the rights in the pending/granted application. These proceedings are expensive and time consuming and should be avoided if possible.

So, it should go without saying that there is now a new urgency to get that filing in as soon as possible, BEFORE the end that one year grace period.

What about in Europe?

Outside the United States, especially in Europe, many countries are what is known as **absolute novelty** countries. An "absolute novelty" country are those countries that require submitted secrets to have NEVER been previously disclosed. If anyone outside of a non-disclosure agreement (or NDA), or an attorney had access to the secret information or claims, that particular innovation is no longer eligible for rights.

This absolute novelty system is one of the reasons why I stress not disclosing to anyone, again, outside of those with whom one has signed an agreement or retainer that specifies non-disclosure. If an inventor discloses an idea to a third party, he or she has technically lost out on the ability to file in many countries in Europe. For this reason, I'll reiterate just one more time: when an inventor has an idea or invention that he or she believe to be commercially valuable or would add constructively to society, and it makes good business sense to prevent others from competing in that same product or service arena, and/or to sell and license the invention, to monetize it in any other ways one can believe possible, they should always talk with a patent attorney before filing their application!

CHAPTER 25

RESPONSIBLE DISCLOSURE

Although sharing the details of an idea may very well be crucial to proving out a concept, it can also become risky for a patent-seeker. How much information should be revealed? Who should one trust? As I mentioned before, one cannot be careful enough about disclosing their invention and it's secret.

That said, there are oftentimes realities in which the inventor cannot completely build-out an entire prototype of the device or innovation on his or her own. Sure, it's in their head, but they can't necessarily build the full prototype without consulting a third party.

Involving a third party on the road to obtaining a patent is quite common. Perhaps the inventor needs someone to build a prototype and/or test said device or process before (or even after) reaching out for legal guidance.

Nonetheless, a prototype is NOT a required to submit a patent application. Yes, that's right: one does not need to have a prototype or working model or even an app before completing the patent application submittal process and receiving a patent pending status on the work. Many inventors don't realize this, and that's why, number one, I recommend having an application submitted BEFORE talking with a third party. Now, if that scenario is either not financially in the cards or is not part of a feasible timeframe, the second best option is to get a nondisclosure agreement (NDA), also called a confidentiality agreement.

These agreements contractually bind either both or one of the parties from disclosing confidential information to any individual or entity that has not also signed an NDA. These agreements are relevant, for example, in software application development. For example, if a certain party develops a brand new business method for social media. The inventor has all of the steps for this new approach in their head and can write it down step by step. They just don't know how to actually do the coding. So, they engage a third party to develop their concept into a working app: someone to put the coding together, get all the systems together and develop it.

Obviously, the inventor knows what the invention is, and because they can provide a complete and thorough written description of the idea, the app to implement the idea does not necessarily need to be developed before they approach a patent attorney or even before they submit a patent application. If the timing is right and if the attorney agrees, a nondisclosure agreement can be written up between the developer and the inventor.

Oftentimes, an inventor will establish an entity, usually a limited liability corporation, for example to protect their interest in the invention. This LLC is responsible for initiating the NDA process and entering into a contract with its third party developer. What the developer would promise in return, among other things, is to do the work and agree to assign all of the rights to the application's coding and development be assigned to the inventor's entity.

This is commonly known as the "Work for Hire" agreement within an NDA. Any of the work products, any of the intellectual property that is created as part of the development process—the coding, the changes, and perhaps iterations of the software and the functions, would all belong to the inventor's entity. That way, the inventor is protected from losing or having to share the potential rights that may be earned by any of their intellectual property.

In accordance with getting an NDA signed by any privy third party and the fact that no prototype is required to submit an application, I want to come back around and talk again about the **provisional patent application** and why it is important to get a patent application filed BEFORE talking with the developer at all.

To help illustrate why filing the provisional first can be so critical, I'll stick with the software example. If the software can be explained in great detail, function by function, (i.e. users log into the portal, the portal communicates with the communications network, the communications network then talks with a business exchange, a merchant exchange, and so on) the software application itself and its function as a business method can be written down as an application without it being physically coded or even created in the app store. The beauty of having a provisional filing with the USPTO is that it acts as prior art against all others, allowing the inventor time to develop, test and reiterate.

In this way, the inventor here has won the first to file race and now has one year to file a non-provisional application. During that one year then, an inventor can most certainly can approach a developer to get the thing built, coded, and tweaked to just right, all protected under the provisional filing (for a time) and an NDA that specifically defines the assignment of assets to the inventor's entity.

Now not just the developer can be approached, but any relevant third party, such as investors, other partners, business advisors, a board of directors, etc. These are great individuals to bring in and explain the full functioning of your patent application. One warning, however, is that what you explain after filing a provisional and what you disclose to others, you've got to be careful that what you tell them is limited to <u>only</u> and <u>exactly</u> what was filed in the application and NOTHING more.

If the inventor divulges any new changes or improvements on their work, they open themselves up to another disclosure issue. Instead, as improvements or changes come about that may not have been discussed in your provisional filing, the inventor can file a **secondary** provisional somewhere within the year before the non-provisional is due.

CHAPTER 26

Patentability Analysis Timeline

What's that first step to investigating whether an idea is patentable?

Great question. Recall from Chapter 6 that a patentable design must be **novel**. Is it new? Before declaring a definitive answer to such a question, one should consult with a patent attorney right out of the gate. Keep in mind, however that any given patent attorney, even if they've got technology background, or a masters or doctoral background in the subject of your invention that does not necessarily mean that they know all the latest technologies that are being invented at all times.

Most likely, the patent attorney may have been in practice a number of years and could very possibly be a little out of touch with the most current or pending patent technologies for their (or their client's) particular field. Not to worry—that's typical. It is not the patent attorney's job (at that moment, anyway) to know whether their client's idea is completely novel. What the patent attorney DOES know, however, is how to conduct a very thorough search and present an expertly informed opinion on whether or not their client's invention is novel. The attorney conducts this search using a specific patentability search methodology. Doing this search is nearly always a good idea. It provides the inventor, business owner or entrepreneur with a set of the closest prior art.

As defined in Chapter 5, prior art works are the similar publications, prior patents that have already been granted and the pending applications that have filed with the USPTO before the new art in question, the prospective invention. Based on specific search terms and query methods—a precise description of which are outside the scope of this book—the patent attorney is able to find out the claims within each of those prior art references to see whether the hopeful invention does, in fact, boast novel claims or whether those prior art claims would potentially prevent the new design from being granted a patent.

The most valuable part of a professionally done patentability search for the inventor is the resulting meticulous and comprehensive expert opinion.

First and foremost, this legal opinion includes whether or not the lawyer recommends to file. Secondly, if they do recommend to file, they can explain the scope of the potential claims that the inventor could make, should the Office call it to issue, based on limitations from prior art.

In the "Real World": Let's use another example of a new invention. It's a different type of skateboard. Just for fun, let's say it has three axles: a front, middle and a rear axle. It's made to undulate with the ground as it shakes—plus, it is fun to ride! Time for the creator to call a patent attorney.

The creator calls a patent attorney that deals with mechanical devices...but they've never heard of this. They really haven't worked on any skateboard type devices before, which I'd say one would expect to hear from most patent attorneys. However, based simply on common knowledge, the attorney will most likely say that the new skateboard seems like a fair idea. They'd like to help with the patent search. The inventor gives them the go ahead and signs on, officially hiring the attorney. The patent attorney does the search...and, lo and behold, there are four different prior art references.

What next?

The attorney must then review these references.

He begins by examining the first three that might be already granted patents.

Two of the three prior art references are from the US and one is from Canada. The two from the US are both similar to the triple axel board, although there are marked differences. The first, say from Orange County, CA only has two axles. However, they both have the same type of flexible board that moves with the ground. The board from Orange County uses the same type of rubber and accordion-like structure that the client described in his drawings, but it is still missing that third axle.

The second prior art reference comes out of San Antonio. It uses the same type of motion as the client's: the claims discuss it. It too, has three axles—but the top is rigid. Moreover, the third axle is not even a real full axle. The third axle in the middle does not touch the ground in normal operation. Instead the wheels on the middle axel are engaged only when performing tricks, like grinding on an edge or half-pipe.

The third example, the board from Canada has four axles, two on the front and two on the rear. The pairs of axels are very close to one another, so there's really no middle axle. Like the example from Texas, it too is made with a rigid top—unlike the client's board which uses flexible rubberized arching.

The last prior is a design application for different ways that the boards could look. One of the drawings is of the top view of a skateboard with a rubberized board feature. It looks to be flexible without the view of the bottom.

After making these comparisons, what might the attorney tell his client?

Truthfully, anything is possible as far as what the attorney could surmise. My goal in this chapter is to give the reader the most detailed possible scenario as a point of reference.

From my experience, with regard to the first two US examples, the attorney would likely conclude that some potentially limiting claims exist. The Californian example, i.e. the one that had the rubberized skateboard top, even though it doesn't have the third axle, seems to work on the same mechanical concepts that use the ground for motion and provide a shock absorption vehicle. The attorney should warn his client that the claims regarding the motion feature of the board may not be able to be patented.

If I were the attorney, I would tell my client to focus his patent goals on the third, center axel. It would also be wise to advise the client to recognize the other areas in which he or she might need to become more flexible, in terms of trying to stake a legal claim.

Then, I would run a search and analysis for each of the priors in order to judge what its effect on the inventors proposed application would be. This will help both attorney and client gain insight as to how broad the rights may be once the application gets to the patent office.

As I always say, it is <u>extremely</u> valuable to do ANY type of patent search.

CHAPTER 27

Additional Resources

On his or her own, and without disclosing the idea to anyone else, before even speaking with an attorney it is advisable to do an initial independent search to see if your idea could be considered novel. This is at least for two good reasons:

1. **Money Saver.** Doing one's own initial search potentially saves you money from having an attorney do a patent ability search; or even worse: having an attorney demonstrate via quick Google search that this idea has already been done.
2. **Knowledge Boost.** Anyone looking to claim legal rights should educate themselves in the field of IP protection. If one does endeavor to write a patent application, knowing more about the USPTO and the particular patent history and/or culture will help the claimant considerably once the decision is made to move forward.

Here are some of the top ways to perform a basic patentability search. And, what's better, they're FREE:

1. **Public Search Engines.** The first step is to use Google or Bing. As many of us know, both Google and Bing are very powerful search engines and contain subject matter ranging from ants to zebras; guns to plush toys, to aliens and Jesus. The internet is full of information. Much of it, unfortunately, is suspect but there are ways to verify sources and certainly there is plenty of useful, wholesome information as well.

   If the search criterion for similar art on Google or Bing comes up dry, provided one has done (at least) a diligent 10 to 15 minute search using different key words, parts and components of your item, different embodiments, and different ways that the invention could look or eventually shape out to be, then this is a pretty good indicator that it is something new for the market.
2. **Google Patent Search.** Another step is to specifically use what is called the Google Patent Search. Type "patents" in the Google search bar and one of the first results will be the "Google Patent Search". Click on it. The page looks very similar to the general Google search page except it will have the word "patents" in gray text just behind the search box. Go ahead and type in those same types of keywords. The results will be only patent literature. They may be international patents,

applications that are pending or granted and issued patents. The difference between this search and a traditional Google search is that it is more refined. One is not sifting through millions and millions of results of unfiltered information, but exclusively searching patent literature.

In fact, the Google Patent Search is one of the first tools that I use when I start a patentability search. The search is open to inventors in the same way. Review the results and look for any prior art that comes across as strikingly similar. Document any findings and bring ALL of the results to a registered patent attorney. They may be able to use this independent search and thus reduce the price in terms of labor required to do a patentability search from scratch.

3. **Advanced Patent Search.** Google also has what's called an Advanced Patent Search. This one I use regularly. Type "advanced patents" in the Google search bar and hit "Enter". A link appears to a new window with an advanced search request form with a number of different fields: patent number, title, inventor, original assignee, and different US classifications, international classifications, patent types, the date range, and issued restricting dates.

   All types of different searches can be performed here and Google is pretty sharp when it comes to searching patent information, so it is definitely worth using for an independent search.

Add a city to the search or try a colleague's last name to see what may come up. One can put in terms and, through Boolean searching, exclude certain words, add one or more words or search an exact phrase. In the same manner as with other search engine results, document anything that looks or acts similar to the new design.

4. **Free Patents Online.** Or www.freepatentsonline.com is a very powerful resource. While this book does not explain all of the details on how to use this tool, I recommend anyone interested in applying for a patent to have a look. There are a wide range of search options available from this resource. One thing I like about Free Patents Online that I will mention is that it is extremely quick and puts a lot of information right at the researcher's fingertips. Once the searcher has obtained a patent number or an application number and enters it into the main search field, he or she can expect to get very quick, specific results.
5. **USPTO.gov.** Another source for do-it-yourself patent searches is the USPTO's website: uspto.gov. They have a lot of newest material. After the AIA (American Invents Act) was passed in 2011 the USPTO received quite a bit of funding[15] and so the site has really come a long way: good information on almost any IP related topic, including all of the topics in this book, is covered to some degree. There is also a very good search reposito-

15 35 U.S. Code § 42

ry in simply doing a basic or an advanced patent or mark search.

6. **PatentLens.** Find this resource at www.lens.org/lens. This site searches the World Intellectual Property Organization, or the entire international application database for potential prior art. This is also a free and open source search for anyone who is interested in learning about the current technology patent hopefuls. This is an AWESOME place for an inventor to find information before talking with a patent attorney.
7. **Patent Scope.** See www.wipo.int/patentscope/en. This database provides access to the International Patent Cooperation Treaty applications in the full text format on the day of the publication.

It is clear that there are plenty of very useful resources for any inventor to use when researching at the pre-attorney stage.

Keyphrase: “GoBigGoBold”

Good for ONE Free 30-minute Consultation with Bold IP Patent Attorney, J.D. Houvener (a $225 value)